Jennifer

Thanks

for

Sculpting

COA.

73

Hello. It Doesn't Matter.

CZ

Derrick C. Brown

Write Bloody Publishing
America's Independent Press

Los Angeles, CA

C. Brown, Derrick.
1st edition.
ISBN: 978-1938912825

Cover Design by Zoe Norvell
Interior Layout by Madison Mae Parker
Proofread by Sarah Kay
Edited by Anis Mojgani, Cristin O'Keefe Aptowicz, Sarah Kay,
Brandon Jordan Brown, & Jeremy Radin
Additional Edits by Aly Sarafa, Amber Tamblyn, and Rebecca Gillespie
Author Photo by Amy Marie

Type set in Bergamo from www.theleagueofmoveabletype.com
Printed in California, USA

Write Bloody Publishing
Los Angeles, CA
Support Independent Presses
writebloody.com

To contact the author, send an email to writebloody@gmail.com
MADE IN THE USA

TABLE OF CONTENTS

PROLOGUE

PROLOGUE

HELLO. BONES.

You, Dear, are my death,
and I'm scared—closer to you,
softening each day.

PART I

THE FIRST SKINNY DIP

Are you sure, Jo?

Before she answered,
her sleek, naked body vanished
into the night waters of Key West.

Her body—
a summer luxe,
unfair,
dragging ivory piano moonlight
into the sea with her.

Careful, Jo.
I see lightning bursting
about a mile to the horizon.

She laughed and swam farther out, away from
the back deck of the old Chris-Craft,
watching me become smaller.

I had missed the sway and rock of my former little ship, The Sea Section.
The best August sway and noon naps of my life.
The worst damp winters of my life.

Hours earlier we roared the Super Chief through the hot Florida rain
until the island Keys ended
and we arrived at our dumpy but sturdy little ship rental
to sleep on for the night.

This is a bad idea. Storm's closing in. Electricity and water, it's so dumb to...

Jo's blond hair
salt-slicked back
just her eyes
exhorting.

I took off my shirt, standing in swim trunks,
embarrassed of my tour body,
my hands octopussing
around the ashamed drink tickets of my gut.

What's the jellyfish situation?
Aren't you freezing?
Do you want your bottoms?
I've never done this before.

Jo laughed.
"You've never skinny dipped?
You gotta just jump in. Live a little.
There's no one out here."

I hate being naked.

"C'mon. You look fine."

I was glad she didn't say amazing.
My trunks slinked to the deck.
I counted to three and jumped stiff, legs out, paratrooper style.
The water, a sloshing chalkboard. The night, cracking.

She came to me,
lifevesting around my shoulders.
"See? Not so bad."

It feels kind of good.
I am worried a fish is gonna swim up my ass,
a little dirty fish. I'm worried we're gonna get fried by lightning.
Tell me Jo, how do you not care?

"I used to be a scared person. Then bad stuff.
Maybe 'cause I've been through so much bad.
I think you are either free after tons of bad
or you are living pre-bad
and have no idea of the bad that awaits you.

I'm French pressing the shit out of every good drop
of the rest of this life."
The night air was nothing.
She hung on me and I didn't sink.
The lightning, flashbulbing in the distance.

LITTLE BONES

I hate your hair in my mouth.
I miss your hair in my mouth.

Full blast is your lighthouse voice box.
You are a solution to the meandering story.

The outboard engines of madness throttle.
My ships seize.
But there you are,
skating upon the freezing surf.
Summoning new seasons.

Summer concedes to your eyes.

Welcoming me,
a kind home.

ESTONIAN ISLANDS AND THE GREAT SHAMPOO CALAMITY

Eventually, we are all bored by elegance.

The entire world fits on my ten-dollar shower curtain.
Makes me feel close to thousand dollar Tahitian dawns
and the Cook Islands don't seem impossible
when I'm soaping up my knees, neighbors of South Africa.

I shower into pure gloss,
skin-hot, bubble stubble,
power-washing my face
and flooding the shores of Estonia.

Dry off by rolling on the clean, white comforter.

The bed is higher 'cause I bought risers
to fit more crap under it.

I see your little desert-busted ankle boots
and holy kid blankets,
winter uniforms all stanked in must
and I can't sleep here
and I love your crap
and I can't make a bed without you—

the fitted sheet is a one-person nightmare.

I stare at my shower curtain map.
In Greenland, my eyelash is a six-hour drive.
In Luzon, my elbow demolishes a quiet beach.

This is a heavy, massive world
that I'll never get old enough to see
in its entirety. I want to. I'm too poor.
I solved desire too late.

I try to tell my hair to wait and not leave me for Easter Island
and it doesn't listen.
It leaves me too soon too.
I tried to work overtime to afford to see
the Corn Islands of Nicaragua,
but I spent it on a drone that also left
as I fumbled the controls.

I curl in your old spot.
I swear I didn't touch your stuff.

Tasmania is fading in the downpour
as a man punishes his neighbors
four times a day, singing too long,
calling for you across this tiny world,
missing the steamed out morning duets.

Come home
and dream of getting lost
for good.

YOU WERE ONCE THE SIZE OF A THUMB

I tried to convince everyone
my heart was a golden rosary,
but I found out it was just anal beads.

Gimme a chaos.

I am vessel lost. Eater of dead starlight. Clear as a cult.
I paid attention to the breeze and I am broke for it.
I am energized by darkness, like a reporter's voice.
I forget everyone I meet was once thumb-sized and pure.

Gimme pure chaos.

I need a champion who can curse like a savior.
I need a job.
I'll need a new job when I get that job.
I am a job, and you can do this job on drugs.

I was once thumb-sized.
Then, the size of a potato sack wishing for a waterbed.
I thought the waterbed would never get old. It did. I did.
I lived proud and alone on that holy sea. My raft of small weapons
couldn't stop the Angel of Eternity from running me aground.

I continue my savior hunt. If he bleeds, he leads.

If I am lost at sea, I would like to know. Gimme a signal.
I know you paint a bicycle white and chain it to the spot where
the rider died.
Be more careful with each other.
Why do I feel at home in a city full of white bicycles?
I sail on in a city of white bicycles.

A woman full of resurrection reaches for me: Are you my rescue?

When she leans in, drunk, *kiss* sounds like *chaos*.
Gimme a chaos, Derrick. Gimme a big fat chaos.
Her hailing eyes.

I see the violent future
and I belong to it.

PORCH HUSHIN'

I once hung

flowers
from the ceiling fan
for my tired love

The room slowly spun in fragrant Rosa Eden
and that gesture was my heart and marrow
and the heart is not enough

So I burnt mesquite and deserts to rid the room
of her morning stretch dance
nap coos and sensible flats
I just want to feel
good enough again
to face the ocean

Diving onto my knees
brings blood
but no forgiveness

I thought I wanted a last love
but I just wanted
souvenirs

The avocado of my heart — so plucked and harsh
doesn't have much time left to ripen

On your beat-up porch, moonlight fails and I tell you
I forgot how to learn someone's favorite color
We're nervous as dogs under bottle rockets

The songs inside me darken when I am alone too long
The windows into my *teen truth* are painted over
All I have choked on is held ransom by the same river guide
punting around in my lower liver
I want to say, Knives up
Hurry up and lunge into me
I don't belong here
I don't understand anything on the radio anymore

I try to crack a joke when you ask me what I want
but you shush me like a sad church
The fan on your porch
spinning the night air out to the tall grass

hushing the skeeters away
A fighting heartbeat
hanging in there
refusing the dull silver of yesterday

LOON

lunar animal
goon my all in the ruin of night

raw horizon
a rise of garage doors opening thigh high

peer at the families of just legs
no one can fit their car in the garage anymore

hold me soon
make room

cactus fruit suck
thirst bust hoot-fresh

body a bottle of gas station champagne
so many ships to christen

her   toes   spread
when I kissed her into the palisade

not a snowy evening carriage slowing
a carjack Cadillac full of blood

kissed her so hard
her mother's eyes still bleed

LOVE IS A MIDNIGHT THUNDERSTORM

A kiss like that
is a breakthrough
the same way a gray whale
breaching right as a strobe of lightning erupts
sees herself in the water before the belly flop and thinks
Holy shit I'm huge
How long have I been this beautiful

Two nude swimmers in the distance, cheering

Help me remember when I complain that I had a leg buckling kiss once
I marvel at my losses too often and forget
we are alive for 12 seconds—
brief as the last flare zigging up
dying at the floorboards of God
hoping for lovers to reunite before the credits

No one can tell me what love is
It's a midnight thunderstorm
and it's as lame as a cheese knife present

It is horny pajamas
watching someone more talented than you
vacuuming in peace
a fresh batch
of fat nasty breaking open the sea

It is seeing leg braces
lying on the beach
with no one in sight

NIGHTSTAND MUSIC

Your flight suit
unzipped in a heap
Deadly legs smoked in jet fuel
Leather gloves undoing my spine

Where'd you come from?
You point up
face all pleased and haunting like a trophy

Tits tightening stiff in my suck
An orchard in napalm

Strengthen my tongue into you
Not drag, but drink
rose water fresh
bursting across your lazy lips

You may love your family
but you are from nowhere when cumming
Master me
Squeezing your feet as your grind out a month of loneliness into me
Fragrant pusher—
a meadow of color in your cheeks
a force of tingles rising as my tongue slides up the center of your
golden hours

Sweat of eyeliner
All the linen erased

Scream out like a movie theater fire
Open the windows
Let the lost tune in
Legs long as a week in Huntsville
Transmit the power
Trigger willows to explode

Out-sass the purple jacaranda, botanical elegance, immoral and fine
The great salted butter of letting go
A laughter of one absurd body learning an absurder body
Prey upon me
Devour this crumbling that longs to destroy you
nightly

Your bra twist-torn and broken free
Never notice the nightstand music
Everything outside is on fire or frozen stiff
A moan to break the snow

DEEP COVER

BEST THING SHE SAID WHEN WE MET
You dress like a narc.

WORST THING SHE SAID AFTER SEX
I hope we're okay.

BEST THING SHE SAID AFTER SEX
I don't want to even be on this planet anymore.

WORST THING I SAID AFTER SEX
Do you happen to appreciate close-up magic?

BEST THING SHE SAID TO MAKE ME FALL IN LOVE AFTER
MONTHS OF SEX
It was so good, you almost knocked out my mouth guard.

BEST THING WE SAID AFTER IT GOT WEIRD
Together or apart, we will be okay.
Let's have a rule where we get high before any heavy discussion from
now on.

BEST THING I SAID AS HER FACE TURNED TO SORROW
WHILE SHE OFFERED ME MUSHROOMS
You are actually under arrest.

THE CORAL SNAKE HATES HIS NECK

I miss my teeth in the flesh
of her low, dune-brown shoulder
Tooth loosed from sucking

I miss our psycho glide
booze sweat deep push howler dawn

A classic Dunkin' Donuts commercial
had these old men hollering
Time to make the donuts!
To me it always meant, It's going to get rough
but let's get to work
In the army, when I'd load my ammo
and fire hundreds of munitions down range
I'd yell out, Time to make the donuts!

You stare at me from across the room
and it is time to make the donuts

Brute necking, blunt force longing
Hold you tight until the shame of body is killed
I turn into a coral snake with so much color and venom
Monitor your heat, steal your young
as the wrestlers on TV trade sweat and looks

Wish they would just kiss already

Miles Davis plays on the cheap record player
sound of the roughshod lifted, brass rising
as the men clench in pixels, mouths close in war

The furnace is
humming along to
Here Come da Honey Man

Your eyes, soft as a benedict
convincing me morning will return in drag
and save us
A sun dyed purple
that hot jagged red smile appearing
Its yellow dress lost in the woods
songing forth from the horizon with quivering light
thrust through these broken blinds
warming us into fast luminance
A shine of bayonet
through pigs
delicate as a tartelette crust
soft and wanting
as dough

THE BODY AS JULY

Grateful for the way we once walked through the pines
You were apologizing to the boughs and needles
with gentle heels
noticing the light warming one side of the conifers
Capturing the way moss sneaks to live on in the dark bark
Tiny holes, vacant homes, thanking the ferns
harmonizing the body with the poplar

I tried to live this way

I am from plywood and Datsun noise
skate ramps and shitty forts
You are from purple milk thistle and where storms are born
running high in the Santa Lucia green
with black nightgown whipping
I watch you fall in the coastal fields—
a credit card flopped on a poker table
laughing like it's all going to be okay

Snowbank smile, calling the condors down
Come lay with me
Hands grace over my jeans like parlor magic
Come home with me
I volunteer to disappear in your bed
Your sheet-mess reveals the chaos in your mind
Come

I lay there as you snore slight and pleased
You sleep like a sailor giving in to the sinking
I stare up in a palace of confusion
scared to move—guerrilla stillness—rigid on a pile of loaded
machine guns
I need an arm across you all night
but don't want to wake you;
you are so kind when rested

The memory deck shuffles:
The eyes made fantastic by the man in Morro Bay
who told you the neon truth
of how your face lit up the entire liquor store

The slugging train through the woods as you napped in my lap
doused in Moscato and mumbling about your strained friendship
with the raccoons

The daylight you screamed into as I screwed you in the rowboat
hoping love would burst from your neck
and waiting

The mini golf I let you win and the bad nachos down your chin
that you couldn't feel

The Joshua Tree shadows I bled under as you squeezed my cock
dumb like a lemon

The bbq wing smoke in Palm Desert and the hot tub wind
that tried to warn us

The man in New Orleans
who told us how lucky we were to be in love
and how I wanted to tell him the Russian sounding sadness of *not yet*

Black birds swing down and pick over carcasses

The deck goes blank

Pringles and vibrators by your bed;
do I still make you lonely?
You stir, turning on your side
Warm machine—more than a healer—
daughter of a nail gun
holding down the roof of the crumbling family home

You turn again
sunlight unlacing across you
The coconut oil on your thigh sheens away
Fingers dawdle in long black fatal hair

I am obsessed with the harmony in these sleeping collarbones
bridges of alabaster
looking down to the shocks of fingernail paint chipped

The body is such a July

My fingers now to your jaw, agape
moving it slightly, puppetting forth the phrase
I love you boy
until you wake and say, "What are you doing?"

Waiting

for you to wake—
Coffee?

PART II

THE AWFUL SOUND OF PACKING TAPE

Boxes being built are a terrible sound—
a brown, temporary sad.

She bought a lot of small boxes.
I wonder if she is moving into a place with stairs,
but I don't get to know anything anymore.

The men humming at her new place begin pulling up
in their horndog motorcade.
She is unpacked, without electricity, and she is free.

I hear the 4am housewarming parties starting across town.
The skinny musicians line up and sing into her mouth.
So many small boxes.

Boys, if anyone spots my snowplow keys in there,
a gold tooth with a moon etched on it,
or something I said in an everlasting tone,
please ring me at the abandoned luncheonette of roaming men.
719-266-2837

ISLAND BREAKS

The amber-colored starfish clings
to the rock he desperately loves.
The sea lion is a dog with no master,
slipping into the blue soaking light.
The tide waltzes the grand monotony.
Thickets of kelp sway—
your ex-lover's hair, deep in the bath.
No, it is not.

It is not what you miss, it's a simple, slow fish.
The striped bass puffs his old man pout
and you recall how she is sad to watch you go for the weekend.
Not really.

The garibaldi drift like gold flakes in a liquor bottle.
They are not her eyes.

The horn shark, all snaggled and heavy, moves alone and
this is not a reminder of the pathetic way you press all your dead-
weight into the bar.

The pink abalones are all shined up on sunlight;
this is not the soft folds of her you miss tasting.

Birds call.
There is nothing to miss about her laugh.

The sheepshead fish lets its red belly blush;
it is not the same good and lost feeling of blushing
naked in our first night.

The spiny lobster, with his long spear, points the way
to the surface and you pretend it is the way home and
do you want to know the way home?

You hike and all the black rocks you carry
are not memories, are flints waiting and
you need to set a fire

to live again

and place your hands in the buckwheat, bud,
because it is alive: the rising silver lotus, the heavy
island oak, the live forever, the fields of locoweed,
screaming bush poppy, sway-away of paintbrush,
island nightshade—proud and breezing, the ironwood is as
alive as the song of the storm petrels, which
is the sister song of the cormorant auklets,
Song of the black oystercatchers, island jays, soft logger-head shrikes, horned
larks, orange crowned warblers,
all the song sparrows hollering to rise.
That's the song of you, bud: the song of all sparrows
who cry serene for love, unprecedented love
in a hymn of repose
knowing
they don't need to know the way home.

WAVERUNNER! NICE WAKE!

My neck skin
thin as a duck's foot.

The Meatman's swap meet switchblade pressed close to the apple.
A mugger's breath is always dry,
radiator wheeze up my spine.

Mad that he was on a fixed-wheel bike—
robbing me while straddling his cool bicycle.

I see him all the time.
Every dream turns into that same mugger's blade
wanting in.

My dreams start so fun.

The WaveRunner, launching across the Texas wake, gave me joy.
The eager dogsled in Fairbanks, huskies snow-eating while
running, gave me joy.
The rope swing into Lake Travis, the letting go, gave me joy.
You wanting freedom over the warmth of my arms gave me joy.

Then, Meatman arrives.
Always from behind.
His favorite knife, *fwwitt* opening to my neck in the Hackney streetlight.
I don't move—then a foreign, tiny scream
comes out of a new hole in my throat
whispering out like a balloon tightened: hEEEEEE
I gurgle in the dirt.
He has dress shoes on. He has dress shoes on...

When you blow-dry your hair and nap after the ocean,
there is joy.
When your lover makes you correctly cooked steak, there is joy.
When you can finally sleep all the way through the night—

then realize you're still in the dream,
Sunday shoes, click click click, coming for you down Shacklewell.

Pockets full of treasure: a twenty-dollar Target watch,
an empty billfold, six Brit pounds and a Texas license,
a blank pocket notebook where the first page says:
If found, lose.

I WISH I COULD HAPPEN AGAIN

I wish I could happen again.
I wish I could happen to someone
again.

I wore your breath till stripped
of its warmth. It's just mine now.
I notice my mouth opens lazily when running—
throat trails out, sounds like animals
exhaling from under the bed.

Who follows me? Who comes after me?
A stupid beast sneaks up on me poorly,
yelling nonsense.

Why listen to the blues
when the blues can't stop listening to me?
Your eyelashes are spider gams.

I wanna die next to you and take your laundry room warmth.
I want to draw the last part of me you loved.

The ocean before us—
the dark mane of an unbroken foal.

I am there.

The weak kid inside wants to negotiate out—
it is all too much. My ribs hurt from not laughing.

I am not safe.
I am the teeth around your nipples waiting
for you
to say when.

Your long black socks, two rivers of night
easing down into the subterranean.
My hunger is the hunger of the mad ones,
the ones without counsel, without family,

without godsend, without love,
with sudden blows to the ribs.

I am empty enough.

A quarry gutted, but so ready
to be turned into a lake, overflowing,
like a dumpster
pushed down the street,
littering pieces
of irrepressible laughter.

HOW CAN YOU HATE ORANGES?

Romance is
calling a neck
a throat

I am too romantic to leave the camp of my past

There is little romance in the far future

Everyone, sad as a straight edge yacht party
Fun as unfolding a broken Kirkland beach chair
Numb as a zookeeper

A sky full of beautiful options
and everyone drugged by
the look down

I try to yell out:
I don't love someone
but rather prefer them!

I tried to smell the roses
at 55 miles per hour—
tried to do-si-do
and swimming hole it up
from a couch with an HTC virtual headset on

The chrome internet conjured friends for me
One of them is a sword swallower

Never bring a sword swallower oranges
Esophagus all nicked up and prone to the burn of citrus
His long *throat*
hiding the scars of entertaining by doing something stupid

He is losing gigs
Everyone is well-read and all about reducing risks
Swallowing a sword is too real to seem real anymore
He convinces me that it's all changing
and that poems by idiots
hold more public fascination, are more lucrative
than those from the dying constant chest miners

I think of all I have hidden from the audience
to stay safe: my fear of being no good, of selling out, of trying too hard

He tries to convince me to sneak a few stupid poems into my next book
Poems mistrusting of any sentiment
Poems that state wants plainly and hastily
A book where I sneak in corporate affections
so I can stay alive

I say "No thanks
I know me
thanks to ancestry.com
and it's just never been in my blood"

THE BUTTER

I want to be the blade
but I'm the butter.

A dog is locked in the car in the parking lot. Windows up.
Devil is talking. Break the windows with my skull. I do,
but the dog doesn't leave.

Freddie Mercury is singing on the TV. Pro moustache.
I am jealous of his tights and courage. I want to break free.
To smash my skull into the glowing box and be gorgeous.
But everything I want to say comes out as a country song.

Hello walls. How'd things go for you today?

The kids on my street invited me over, pinned me down and lit
my hair on fire.
I tried to swallow the batteries in the remote. I tried the remote.
Too many channels.
Shins first onto parking blocks.

Heart huge and gut gorgeous and knees nasty. Sweat and faults
and Freddie comes out of my hair and says he misses the sing-along.

I HAVE:
- a solid emotional support system of friends, family, and/or
  professionals that I can use if I feel like Skulling.
- at least two people in my life
  that I can call if I want to let all the light in.
- at least three different people who are somewhat comfortable talking
  with me about Skull Smashies.
- a list of at least ten things I can do instead of head thrusting into glass.
- a place to go if I need to leave my house
  so as not to head burst.
- confidence that I could get rid of all the things
  that I might be likely to use to go Skull Lancing.
- told at least two other people that I am going to stop
  being a goddamn ram.

- to feel uncomfortable, scared, frustrated,
  bloody and warm.
- assurance that I can endure thinking about Smashy Smash without
  having to actually do so.
- to stop the devil.

I WILL:
- slash an empty plastic soda bottle
  and wait for rain to have a regatta race.
- make a soft cloth doll to represent the voodoo inside.
- flatten aluminum cans for recycling,
  seeing how fast I can go.
- never turn them in.
- hit a punching bag that is dressed for success.
- use a pillow to hit a wall and wait for the wall to say
  Hello. It doesn't matter.
- rip up a phone book when no one calls.
- on a photo of myself, mark in red ink where I need Smashies.
  Cut and tear the skull.
- throw ice into the bathtub or against a brick wall
  hard enough to shatter it and yell skulllllll!
- put my finger into ice cream for five minutes
  until both change.
- bite into a hot pepper or chew a piece of ginger root.
- rub liniment under my nose.
- slap a tabletop, hard.
- snap my wrist with a rubber band.
- take a cold bath.
- stomp my feet on the ground and wait for it to break.
- focus on how it feels to breathe. Notice
  the way my chest and stomach move with each breath.
- eat a blueberry mindfully.

How does a blueberry smell? Notice that I'm beginning to salivate, and see
how that feels. Are there little seeds or stems? How is the inside different from
the outside? Finally, swallow.

It's the devil.

LIKE A DUMPSTER FULL OF FLOWERS

You thought these images were just for poetry workshops:
A sky full of surrendering bodies.
An ocean of lost letters.
A dumpster full of roses.

Then you see it.

A long green dumpster, four feet tall,
flowing with fresh and old flowers.
Daffodils and carnations, plastic leaves, roses galore,
some in grand wreaths, some with names still on the easels in petals.
James in styrofoam. Tara on a beauty queen banner.
Stefanie under a photo of Stefanie.

A long dark photo album
overflowing with flechettes and shrapnel of scattered color.

I go to a funeral every year now.
I tell my friend to not waste his money on flowers.
He says it makes him feel a little better
to throw away a few cards, some money, some food,
pour out some good whiskey, let it go to waste,
because he doesn't know what else to do.

SEAM. STRESS.

I looked up her new boyfriend on the internet.
He posted a new set list with her name on it.
He wrote her a song. Already.

I shouldn't have looked. The child in my blood.
I texted her that she deserves all the songs.

Goddamn.

All light holds a grudge and wants to undo the shade.
Later that night, it begins to hail.
Jesus has a kink in his neck. Can't see me.
When you are sad
the dumbest thing you can turn to
is a puzzle.
When I can't solve a Rubik's Cube,
I break it into pieces
and often just leave it that way.

I go online again.

Another ex posts her marriage license.
Another, her law degree.
Another, their new dogs on vacation.

I post a picture of an okay pancake.

SPRING WHACK

you buy a suit
and wait for someone
to love you

you try and engage with the world
but there is someone more interesting
at the party

the slow dread of surprise snow
when you woke early and took a chance
on shorts

have you seen it snow in the sunshine?
the laggy-slide-away ice death
of everything losing its grip

wanting
is like crying
to a song you hate

PART III

GIGGIN' FROGS

The frog gigger is a rod with a tiny bear trap on the end
If a flower hits it right
it will snap down all hasty and kill that flower

I get close to the frogs at night
and their eyes glow demonic
in my headlamp

They can't see each other
so they cry out to each other
croaking through nightfall

Sometimes land and sometimes water
I have to stop obsessing
about living in two worlds

I never catch them
I'm too slow
and too mystified when near

I look up and focus my energy into the phone lines barely visible overhead
I try to *will* my father to wonder about me, maybe call on his own
To tell him he taught me well and that I won't starve

I open my mouth towards the baby powder moon
croaking away all night
hoping to supper alone on the legs of the soon quiet

LOST IN LISBON

The great city sends its yellow trolleys into the hills,
blocks of butter retrieving lovers.

Black and white tiles snaking across sidewalks
shuffle me into the docks where Portuguese coffee warms
and red bridges stretch wide as a young mother's arms.
The tight washing light blowing in from Sintra,
a hard, smooth spreading of warmth,
salt air lifting a mad language.
The ceviche orgasm.
The sound of desperate fado,
                              splitting the body
like farewell sex.

How blessed to be a city not in the news.
You are easy when you are forgotten.

EVENING OF TEL AVIV DANCERS

The dancers are at rest
on stage, rolling around like toddler slobs,
like they've all just been broken up with
in sweatpants and dirty socks,
burying the beautiful body under layers.

The music lifts
and there they go, resistance and slinking grace
slowing, shedding until warm,
revealing miracles and pleas within the body,
unashamed and wowing the air.

The choreographer pushing them:
I need your arm to bend more like a swan's neck.
I need your leg to curl tighter, more nautilus.
I want your teeth to clench when you lift her…
and no one asks why.
They just do, soldiers of young trust.

Can you watch three dancers without imagining
it is the story of an affair?
Two dancers tumble around on each other like rolling pins
as the third steamrolls offstage.
Looks like they worked it out.

Israeli dancing women with jet black brows,
crows exhaling over a soft Negev,
ponytails like vines whipping in a jungle storm,
arms sleek as bike frames,
cement humor,
psych synth accent,
and uneasy about the world.

My ticket was in the back of the theater.
"So you can keep an eye on the audience and the show.
Your enemies are all around you."

CRAZY WE DON'T THINK
THERE'S PAIN IN BARCELONA

in Barcelona, you slept with your clothes on
flattened by flamenco and Iberico ham
pressed into the bed like flowers in a journal
a page you'll never open to again
your colors compressed
your hair distressed
a person photographed in a storm
but your face
the pillow holding your God face
the marvel of a human doing nothing perfectly
killing me in the sheen and beams
of ignored TV light

HOW TO BE A BETTER STRANGER

Every dog I meet thinks I'm a celebrity.
I wish I could treat everyone I meet like I was a dog:

I would get nervous and ask too many questions,
so attentive, brilliant storytelling,
instead of seeming so weary and hard of hearing.

We could talk about the weather or the worst rap of all time.
Is it "Eyes Without a Face" or "The Man from Mars"?
We're both right! I love you!

If I can respect groceries, bone marrow, and mystery treats,
I can respect learning a new person's past.

I could sniff your ass
to see if you're depressed.

I either sat in lipstick
or the past keeps kissing my ass. So many smells.
I want you to touch me so bad,
I could piss all over the floor.
Elation is yellow.

HOW TO LOVE YOUR SMALL TOWN

You can go to Aviator Pizza for great beers and flat pizza right off the highway. Enjoy the conspiracy theories at the Liberty Tree bar. The wine ain't bad at The Owl and they have an open mic where two or three people usually sign up and shame Jason Aldean. Parker Lumber is your neighborhood tool joint and Bloomers nursery has everything to get your garden ready for dinner. I am trying to remember the times I'd go to the Coupland Dancehall—

I think we died there.
It's fuzzy.
It's like trying to forget a song you love.

Our town is pronounced Elgin like "Again," due to a Scottish railroad owner moving the railroad from Bastrop to "Hogeye" and renaming the town after himself. You can watch sports and get a good, thick hot dog at Regulator's. There's a tiny, secret country bar called Type Store that only has beer in cans in a woman's living room.

Sometimes I heard wild dogs running,
growling hunger through the grass behind me.

There's a drive-through beer barn that has a few craft beers. Anytime Fitness is rarely crowded. Domino's delivers way out here, but that's it. Cele Store BBQ is cozy on Friday and Saturday and...

and... I can't remember what I was trying to be...

The Good Luck Grill has dinner and horseshoes and washers. ShadowGlen is a golf course only about 15 minutes away. 1660 is the best drive from "Hogeye" into Hutto, you will feel so much.

Like you could settle down in the middle of nowhere
and lose your friends.

Coffee Catz drive-through has okay coffee and snow cones. Tons of films shot around here: *Bernie. Transformers. What's Eating Gilbert Grape. Varsity Blues. Friday Night Lights. Texas Chainsaw Massacre.*

Make yourself at home. Love the quiet.
Polaroids fading fast, kill-light of the sun.
You and I danced and died in the coastal Bermuda grass.
I loved you in conspiracy and Miller Lites.
I loved you in the scoot of your boots.
I loved you madly, but not forever.
A small town letting go, changing little.

Subscribe to the *Elgin Courier*, original paper, 200 years old.

Sometimes I thought a stray dog was chasing me outside of town but the neighbor said he swore it was Lucifer, poised as a black dog with a shine to his coat. I told him I thought that dog was trying to kill me. The neighbor said, "Nah, he just wants to be fed."

DERRICK C. BROWN:
ENTREPRENEUR OF THE YEAR

I'm a 73. Let me start again. I made my millions building a website
that starts off with a lengthy questionnaire:

How many organic cigarettes or cloves do you smoke a week?
How fast did you read *The Things They Carried*?
How many sexy hikes do you take a year?
What is your nightly drink of choice?
What twenty films do you bring to a remote island with power?
Etc.

Then based on your risks in life and your taste,
it will sort out, on average, how much time you have left on this earth
and how many books you can squeeze in to read before you die.

For an added fee, based on your style, it will tell you which books to
end on. We only have so much time and I have wasted half my life
reading books that were just okay.

I only have time left to read 73 books. You're a 256? I never trust a 256.
You're either a damn skimmer or you want to live forever.

FROM 1993-1999 I WAS A BORN AGAIN ABSTINENT MAGICIAN AND I MADE A LIST OF MY STANDARDS FOR DATING SO I COULD GET MARRIED BY THE AGE OF 24

My future wife should:

be either smart or pretend smart
not bribe me to know the secrets to my tricks
run from the house if she sees me pull up
like her dad some
unlock my door if I open hers
delight in good music
be able to go places on her own, no personal curfew
know why she likes something
initiate the kiss or tell me to beat it when I'm desperate
think burps and farts are funny
take me to taco bell when I'm sad
not make me ashamed for praying my way back into virginity
be able to digest the food I make—sometimes just tomatoes
let me lick her face, look at my eyes when we talk,
not be against tackling
have situational awareness,
be willing to dance like an idiot
be willing to make noise when getting back rubs
be a girl that would rather survive than look good all the time
not smoke pot but cloves okay
be a thrill seeker but not suicidal
feel that it isn't work to talk into the night
say thank you to her kill, even fish
never call summer the summer of salads
know what rain is for
be willing/able to sing poorly in front of me

summon new thoughts, no open-toed shoe nights
tell me when my breath is gnar-gnar
talk to the waiter and send back dog crud
not be afraid to ask for a discount
be foxy some
have a body that could influence men in business

DERRICK C. BROWN'S YEARBOOK OF IMPOSSIBLE THINGS

The things I was built out of (MACHINERY)
Couches upholstered in doubt.
A Svengali deck.
John Lucero skate decks.
New Order dancehall squeaking Creepers.
Gun oil and Kiwi shoe polish.
Anne Sexton bouffants.

The reason I was voted worst doctor in the world (SURGERY)
I was only sew-sew as a surgeon. Kill me now.
I tried to heal people with ideas. Couldn't heal myself.

Why they shut my circus down (STRANGE FEATS)
I cried and cried and climbed a tall ladder and jumped
into a tiny cup of my tears. It hurt.
There was already a flattest man on earth.

A short history of the few dreams I can remember (FANTASY)
Someone finally carves my initials deep into a tree
because desire has turned them mad against the trees.
I have 60 seconds to dismantle an orgasm.
I cut the make-me-feel-special wire.
Stacey Dash explains to me the Stacey Dash experience.

I emptied my lover's purse (SMALL NECESSARY THINGS)
I found shortbread.
I found a jar of hot presence
and a small box of detergent to dump into arrogant fountains.
I found a taser set to night night y'all.

The reviews came in from my autobiography (THE PAST)
No thank you was the most popular.
The demands Mr. Brown gave to the police
and his readers still cannot be met.

JUMBO'S CLOWN ROOM IS US

They aren't allowed
to take off their panties.
I'm not sure they really want to.
It's often more gymnastics than stripping.

Erica and I watch the last performer
at Jumbo's Clown Room,
Brandy, in a tassel sparkle bikini and clear 90's pumps,
take the stage like a loosened silk kimono.

Brandy dances and unleashes her panties,
chucks them into the air, catches them, and smiles.
But she has another pair of panties on.
She does this three times. Puts a clown nose on.
The sexiness of zilch fucks.

Brandy removes each panty—the creep show
of that word— with a youth group
magician's panache
and proceeds to juggle them,
and Erica and I think it's love.

Erica and I used to hang out and drink
until one of us began to cry.
Going to Jumbo's was part of the plan
to not sit at pubs all night until breaking.

Brandy heads to the back booth
to grind some goateed production gaffer for 20 dollars
and the guy is trying so hard to pretend to not be hard.
Cocks always trying their best to get attention and ruin someone.

Afterwards, we pull her aside and say, "Hey Brandy,
we loved your… set?" and she puts her hand on my shoulder,
squeezes my awe,
winks and whispers, "My name is not Brandy."
Grinning, Erica and I, mystified, *How do we get there?*

YOU'RE STEWED, BUTTWAD

So, what would you little maniacs like to do first?
- Lisa from *Weird Science*

Eugene Mirman. You have made me a man
in the same way Kelly LeBrock was made a woman by nerds.

Meaning, I was already a man, but you built me up
and encouraged me to use my magic to turn turdy people
into real turds.

Thank you for your wisdom.
Who really knows how wet a whale's vagina can get?
Your answer is: pretty wet.

I now realize declaring that something is the champagne of beers
is like saying the chocolate cake of burritos.

You just found out the horned lizard
shoots blood out of its eyes for defense.
If you could do that at the optometrist,
people would remember your name.

Thank you for silly permission.
For showing me it's okay to confuse the stars.
It's okay to chortle in church.

You're just like Stalin,
if Stalin only murdered sadness.

THE VET

When you need to walk farther than you can see,
no headphones, a weapon in your pocket,
off into the calm teal of nowhere. Go.

When you hear the gangs of night want to put you down
like a whole kennel of hopefuls,
when it calls you to drink steady that slow pink syringe.
Drift.

Walk away into the desert.
Say, Love's not coming home tonight.
It's out dismantling the revenge plague.

Tell the vast list of my dreams to settle down
and relax into a history book,
until overcome with the pressure
of how unnecessary we are.

A JEALOUS GOD HOVERING
IN THE DEAD LIGHTS

Jesus raised another man from the dead besides Lazarus
but this man was an idiot.
The man woke from the heavy slumber and cried,
"There's no heaven!"
The Apocrypha says Jesus laid him back down,
pressed on his neck firmly, very firmly, looking for a "pulse,"
held his hand tightly to the man's lips, felt his dull breath grow faint
and whispered, "False alarm."

ENDLESS FACTORY

At all times
someone somewhere

needs flowers.
I can't keep up.

How do we not run out?
How are there always

always
flowers?

STARS HISS OUT

Am I the only one
who can hear
the stars hissing
across the smooth pond
of night

Where do their
spirits go
when they burn
out

A hiss rises
and the gates open
wobbling into the white ocean
of all dead stars cooling
No more work to do

You showed me
the hole in your gut
where they put
the bag
and it hissed

and I felt the backs
of my knees
tingle and we
said no last words
just imagined

the scene: a heaven
for stars
a place
to let go of twinkling refraction
and turbulence

and finally
unglow away

PEARL OF GREAT PRICE

There is no way to get to heaven
without
hurting someone.

HELLO. SAILBOAT SHEETS.

Everyone loves to visit, but the long hours cold and alone? It's misery.
It is so cold here on The Billy Ocean, the white fiberglass walls
are wet from my breath.

I warm my sleeping cap over the stove pot and place it on my head.
The boat is so small, I washed the chili-coated spoon in the sink while
still in bed. I was going to throw it away but I was too cold to remove
the sheets from my legs. The fish are not biting. The weather makes
me care less about living the dream of harvesting my own food. Wait.
My face is bleeding. My razors have gone bad when I start bleeding.
There is an old bottle of vodka I am afraid to touch because it was left
here by a woman named Mercedes, a beautiful girl with bad taste.
Every night is dinner alone with a silencer bolted to the phone. Why
did I shave before bed? I look at the reflection in the water and I miss
Disneyland Christmas lights. Do I love the sea this much? I drink the
vodka.

I remember, as a little boy, wanting to live among the Pirates of the
Caribbean ride, in the swamp or the boat war scene. One more sip and
I'm there. I can't wait for sunlight to finally come so I can send a few
cannonballs over the bow of the Spanish and make my way to the Blue
Bayou, more blue now than ever. Dancing with women, drinking with
pigs. In a jail, all my dirty friends, who I will someday rescue and
be rescued by.

HELLO. FINISH YOUR WILL.

I tried to write my will in a Miami Cubano bar with my friend Jo.
The idea sounds like a good drinking game:
Think of all your material possessions,
the t-shirts that were souvenirs of a beautiful time become rags,
the thousands of dollars of books
that will sell for 50 bucks total.
The unused knives that made you feel safe,
25 cents a piece at the estate sale.
Your worthless, desperate journals, a chuckle to your married friends.
Who will I gift this stuff that no one wants?
Who can I burden, as a last joke?

I have too much.

I tried to and stopped. I cried spring colors.
As the objects were listed
and the names were assigned,
I shook, uncontrollably.
All these people on the list
are friends.

That much love is an earthquake.

I have so much.

HELLO. IT DOESN'T MATTER.

In my handsome garden I look down from the heavens and you two
are beautiful together and it doesn't matter and you look at her and
see that she's your only truth the wood-splitter of your heart and it
doesn't matter and he's your dream museum your favorite species
marrow sucking apprentice and it doesn't matter and she loved you like
a hidden God and it doesn't matter and he wants no one else but he
sees it in her posture that she might and it doesn't matter and there's
someone better always and it doesn't matter and a bird crashes into
his window he will wonder if the bird is lost or if his window was in
the way but it doesn't matter and her hurt and hate for me is growing
in her liver and it's too large to cut out or she'll bleed to death and it
doesn't matter and he has a violence inside that lives in his sperm and
I put it there and it doesn't matter and she wishes she was designed
better but she wasn't and it doesn't matter and you want her to look
up and love you again to love you harder than sneezing with your eyes
wide open and it doesn't matter and he will wish his season wasn't all
over so soon but it is and it doesn't matter and you'll both wonder why
did I make your ending so grueling and you will hunger to know but I
won't answer
and it doesn't matter

                •

I love you, useless.
Love is not the moon and sun
swapping space. It is one
eating the weaker nightly.
One of you will win.
So just drink your wine and cry
and become a flood.
Drink down all that loneliness.

Sometimes it will feel like it's just
you and me in the garden,
but sometimes, it's really just you.

You thought you two were a church
that couldn't be torn down, a synagogue
that couldn't be unbelieved in.

You'll think, wasn't I designed
for her? Why must we stray?
You will look up and think:

Why don't you just un-design all this grief?
Why won't you just make it go away?

Because it is in me
and I need to be known. I can't go away.
I can never die. Death and loss
are my gifts. If you know
my pain, you can know my love.

I love you in rivers.

MOONPLOSION

Know what level of magic you are on. Command vultures
with invisible kite strings. Make a recipe for grief. Make
a promise to the dirt to visit soon. Stand against the sliding
glass door and watch the tornado do what it has to do and put
your fingers down your storm. Tell the moon it is fat. Mean it
in an ugly way. Body shame the moon. Fight the moon.
Especially on your last day together. Feel every part of the
freeway that is lonesome move through you. Love all your
wanting. Love and wait for the large desire and laugh into
its asshole. Lose motherfucker, lose. Now heron away.

DERRICK C. BROWN IS THE DISNEYLAND OF COMEDY

Come explore
The Success Cemetery

Take a photo in front of
The Museum of False Alarms

Bring the kids to their knees at
the 9pm *Wet Fireworks Show*

Pop on in to the
Stomach Problems in Traffic Food Court

Challenge your lover on the
I'm Fine, I Said I'm Fine, It's Like a Five-Minute Drive Bumper Cars

Don't miss the
Fake Ass Smile, Real Ass Marching Band

Wait in the tremendous line to experience
The Tiny Dancehall for One

Catch a showing of the epic romantic one-minute movie,
The Good Years with You

Challenge your friends at *Dr. Depression's Free Throw Booth*
where my former high school P.E. teacher tells you that you are so bad
you should consider killing yourself.
Prizes for the most misses!

Visit the *Hungover Again on a Flight After You Said You Would Never Be
Hungover on a Flight Again Gift Shop*
where every piece of lost luggage is certified emotional!

Smash it up at
The Interactive Gallery of Suddenly Broken Printers
When You Needed a Printer the Most

Feast your eyes on
The Caricature Portraits of My Busy Friends

Holler on the *Log Ride that Stops Whenever*
The fun is that it could end at any moment!
It's so

NOTES

The poem "Hello. It doesn't matter." was commissioned by super French choreographer Martin Harriague.

The poem "From 1993..." references "the summer of salads." Cristin O'Keefe Aptowicz once called our summer together the "summer of salads," but it was Austin, so it was actually the summer of murder death, murder blood, and murder heat.

The phrase "Crazy we don't think there's pain in Barcelona" is from the song "Barcelona" by Rufus Wainwright.

"Pearl of Great Price" references a religious text I've never read.

There are two poems about dumpsters and two poems about Disneyland in this book, as well as two very stupid poems hidden within these pages. Hunt!

Grateful to The Hatchery Press in Los Angeles and AIR Serenbe outside of Atlanta for their residencies and place to create this work.

Special thanks to Lizzy Ellison for her insight, tips and eternal babeness.

OTHER BOOKS BY DERRICK C. BROWN

How the Body Works the Dark
Uh-Oh
Our Poison Horse
Strange Light
Valentine the Porcupine Dances Funny
Working Mime to Five: Cruise Ship Pantomime Revealed!
I Looooove You, Whale!
Hot Hands and the Weirdo Winter
Scandalabra: Poetry & Prose
I Love You Is Back
Born in the Year of the Butterfly Knife

ABOUT THE AUTHOR

DERRICK C. BROWN is a novelist, comedian, poet, and storyteller. He is the winner of the 2013 Texas Book of The Year award for Poetry. He is a former paratrooper for the 82nd Airborne and is the owner and president of Write Bloody Publishing, which *Forbes* and *Filter Magazine* call "...one of the best independent poetry presses in the country." He is the author of eight books of poetry and three children's books. The *New York Times* calls his work, "...a rekindling of faith in the weird, hilarious, shocking, beautiful power of words." He lives in Los Angeles, California.

BROWNPOETRY.COM

IF YOU LIKE DERRICK C. BROWN, DERRICK LIKES...

BIRTHDAY GIRL WITH POSSUM
BRENDAN CONSTANTINE

SLOW DANCE WITH SASQUATCH
JEREMY RADIN

HOW TO LOVE THE EMPTY AIR
CRISTIN O'KEEFE APTOWICZ

STUNT WATER
BUDDY WAKEFIELD

THE FEATHER ROOM
ANIS MOJGANI

COUNTING DESCENT
CLINT SMITH

DO NOT BRING HIM WATER
CAITLIN SCARANO

Write Bloody Publishing distributes and promotes great books of poetry every year. We are an independent press dedicated to quality literature and book design.

Our employees are authors and artists so we call ourselves a family. Our design team comes from all over America: modern painters, photographers and rock album designers create book covers we're proud to be judged by.

We are grassroots, D.I.Y., bootstrap believers. Pull up a good book and join the family. Support independent authors, artists and presses.

Want to know more about Write Bloody books, authors and events?
Join our maling list at

www.writebloody.com

WRITE BLOODY BOOKS

WRITEBLOODY
QUALITY AMERICAN BOOKS

HIDDEN TRACK

NICK CAVE'S JOURNAL OF IN-BETWEEN SONG PATTER

My ex girl was younger and too into Harry Potter,
she was all about hit it and quidditch.

The hit band The Heights asked the pressing question, "How do
you talk to an angel?" The answer? Eat shit and die.

I would not invest in a glow stick company called That's So Ravin'.

No one's writing sexy worship songs anymore.
Replace the word Jesus in every worship song with Steve.
Now all the songs sound like fantasy fixation mania on poor, sexy
landscaper Steve. Do you know that Steve mowed for your sins?

A moonwalking nazi. Now *that's* reverse racism!

If you get high with actors, shit will get mellow dramatic.

You're not really pro-life until you're getting paid for gigs.

I was caught masturbating as a child. I mean... dressed as a child.

I'm not into horoscopes, but I'm into scopin' whores, dang!

Free whiskey is sexual harassment.

I want to drink a thick smoothie and then use Gwen Stefani's
bathroom just to tell her my shit is, indeed, "bananas."

When two incontinent people fall in love
you should throw them a bed wedding.

I chased a shot of whiskey with a wristwatch.
Now all my time is wasted.

The end. (There you go, Mary.)

CPSIA information can be obtained
at www.ICGtesting.com
Printed in the USA
LVOW03s0038210318
570564LV00005B/7/P